Tales from Over The Moon
The Larkdale Chickens

Would you like a free e-book?

Busy Miss Hoover is now available for FREE on Bookstore.

CassGriffin Publishing
61 Bridge St.
Kingston
HR5 3DJ
United Kingdom

Author: Pauline Dawber
Illustrator: Surya Gunawan

Copyrights: Pauline Dawber
©text   ©Illustrations
Published 2024
All rights reserved

No part of this book may be reproduced in any form or by any electronic or mechanical means including storage and retrieval systems without permission from the author, except in the case of a reviewer who may quote brief passages embodied in critical articles or in a review.

ISBN 9781666407143

iRead youRead

If you would like to receive our latest publication news, other treasures and colouring pages for FREE, sign up for the newsletter on our website.

www.ireadyouread.com

Tales From Over The Moon Series

Busy Miss Hoover   Harold'sTale
Molly Mop and Bucket. Kassuku
The Larkdale Chickens The Fiddler

To

Harvey Carter

Tales from Over The Moon
The Larkdale Chickens

Pauline Dawber

Illustrated by Surya Gunawan

Bury St. Edmund's cattle market is always on a Wednesday.
It is a noisy bustling place.

Herds of people, cattle, sheep, pigs, goats, geese, chickens and rabbits all have their say at once!

Farmers haggle and yell their prices as the hammer goes down.
SLAM!
Metal gates slam shut and slam open.
Weaving your way cleverly through the gaps of people is the best way to see anything at all.

It seems chaotic but the calming spring sunshine is warming the cold, still wintery morning.

Arriving in the market from the quaint town of Larkdale with his family, is a young boy named Harvey.

They have come to buy some geese, chickens maybe a peacock or two, a boat and preferably a yellow Land Rover.

It is quite a shopping list!!

Harvey with his mop of blonde unruly hair, a twinkle in his eye, and sporting his T-shirt " I'm rockin' my extra chromosome", spots Inflatable and Best Hen Friend Tumbleweed amongst the feathered crowd.

The hens are bought at a good price and Harvey knew at once they were the perfect companions for his mischievous plans.

You may remember Inflatable and Best Hen Friend Tumbleweed are good friends of Busy Miss Hoover.
They are no ordinary chickens.
They are nosy, curious and have a liking for adventure.

Harvey is a spirited young boy with Down's Syndrome.
Because of this, there are some extra obstacles for him to jump through and over.

Even so, Harvey loves physical training, playing his trumpet, dancing, and spreading his cheerfulness around to everyone he meets.

Whatever the weather, amid the barley or in the yard, Harvey loves having a lot of farmyard fun!

And so it is, that Harvey finds his match with the two Larkdale chickens.
Little did he know, they were all about to begin a feather-ruffling spree.

As soon as the trio sets foot on Harvey's family farm, the feathers start flying..........
quite simple and plain to see!

Inflatable and Tumbleweed could not resist poking their beaks into everything.

The veggie patch, the tool shed, to pecking on small glass windows and sending the dust flying as they wriggled, jiggled and joggled each other over the space for a dust bath.

It looks as if they are settling into their new home very well.

Inflatable is a plump Rhode Island Red Hen with a liking for popping out of unexpected places, much to the surprise and amusement of everyone nearby.

Tumbleweed, on the other hand, is also a Rhode Island Red Hen but sleek and agile with a talent for acrobatics that would rival any circus performer.

Tumbling, rolling, bouncing and jumping even rolling like the tumbleweed plant on a windy day across the farmyard are the favourites.

The tumbleweed kind of rolling did get out of control now and again, depending on just how strong the Fen wind blew.
However, Tumbleweed only very occasionally needs some Arnica medicine.

The chickens' antics bring a smile to everyone's face from the youngest chicks to the wisest roosters.

Harvey's days begin with the sunrise.
He eagerly rushes to the chicken coop to greet his feathery companions.

Inflatable and Tumbleweed reply with enthusiastic clucks and flaps, signalling another day filled with pranks and joy.

It is time for some farmyard fun.

Harvey sets up a maze made from Grandma's flower pots.
It is an obstacle course for his feathery friends.
Inflatable and Tumbleweed take to it like ducks to water... well, chickens to flowers in this case!

The sight of two chickens handling the maze, (not always that well) has everyone in stitches.

Harvey's pranks didn't stop there.

One day he adorns the chickens with cardboard crowns and declares them,

"Super Cluckers of Larkdale."

Inflatable and Tumbleweed strutt around the farm feeling like heroes.

One Sunday morning, Harvey decides to organise a chicken parade through the town square.

Dressed in mostly paper costumes and Harvey playing his trumpet, he leads the chickens in a procession that had the townsfolk laughing and cheering! The dynamic trio keep the town talking!

Whatever next!

As the days pass the trio's antics only grow better.

Inflatable discovers a love for cartwheels and Tumbleweed perfects a high- flying routine that involves leaping from the coop and landing on Harvey's outstretched arm.

The chickens could not get enough of Harvey's trumpet playing!

They did find time though, to eat lunch with their other feathery friends.

Another famous hen, Henny Penny had heard that the two chickens were in the area and flew in to say hello.

Unfortunately, Henny Penny is still convinced that the sky is falling down and that life as chickens know it, is over.......

The two daredevil chickens suggest to Henny Penny to be brave.
She could look up and check whether the sky is still falling.

One day Harvey notices a gloomy mood hanging over the town of Larkdale.

The yearly harvest festival was approaching but the townsfolk seemed too busy and too stressed to even notice any festivities.

Determined to spread cheerfulness, Harvey joins up with Inflatable and Tumbleweed for a secret mission.

Under the cover of night........ the trio decorate the entire town with feathers and a few fireworks.

They create an exciting, if not slightly unusual, fluffy, downy mixed with fire, wonderland.

As the sun wakes up in Larkdale and the citizens draw their curtains back, they are greeted with this thrilling scene and they all come out to celebrate the Harvest Festival.

The sight of the town transformed into a feathery fiery paradise, lifts everyone's spirits.

The harvest festival becomes the most joyous celebration the folks of Larkdale have ever seen.

From that day forward Harvey, Inflatable and Tumbleweed become local legends.

Their farmyard fun still brings laughter and happiness to the town.

The mischievous chickens continue to surprise and delight. Larkdale is becoming a place where joy and feathers float in the air.

When you visit, you can find a magical feeling that will last for a long, long time.

Meanwhile, Harvey grows up and
moves away from Larkdale.

Eventually, he comes to live in another happy place called
Over The Moon.

Some years earlier, the two chickens had also moved away
to join Busy Miss Hoover and friends on Over The Moon.

Harvey always has his trumpet with him and is delighted
to meet up with Inflatable and Tumbleweed once more.

The trio have much to talk about.
They are still local legends.

The dynamic duo introduce Harvey to Busy Miss Hoover,
Harold, Molly Mop and Bucket, Kassuku and The Fiddler.

You may remember that thinking hats are trendy
on Over The Moon.
Not everyone owns one, but most folks do.

It is a hat that when you wear it you can easily slip
into a quiet time, come back to yourself, do a bit of
daydreaming, and afterwards feel refreshed.

Kassuku has decided that he does not want one, as his
feathers are fine enough.
Inflatable and Tumbleweed have also decided
not to own a hat either.

You can say that birds of a feather stick together!

Harvey is thinking about it!

For the folks who live on Over The Moon, most evenings are spent together around the fire pit.

This evening, the trio have a song to sing.
And a trumpet to play.
Very soon everyone joins in.
The strong voices float through the stars, gathering extra stardust, moving the sounds around the moon and back again.

It is a famous and familiar song, passed down from one long time to another long time.

Old McDonald has a farm,
E- I-E-I-O
And on this farm,
There is a boy
E-I -E-I-O

With a trumpet here
And a trumpet there
Here trump, there a trump,
Everywhere a trump trump,
E-I-E-I-O

And on this farm,
there are some chickens
E I E I O

With a cluck cluck here
And a cluck cluck there
Here a cluck, there a cluck
Everywhere a cluck cluck
Old McDonald has a farm
E I E I O

Old McDonald has a farm
E I E I O
And on this farm, there are some feathers,
E I E I O
With a tickle tickle here
And a tickle tickle there
Everywhere a tickle tickle
E I E I O

THE END

iRead youRead

I hope you enjoy reading about Harvey and the Larkdale Chickens.

Please visit our website
www.ireadyouread.com

If you like colouring in there are some colouring pages with the newsletter sign-up.

Happy reading!

About the Author

Deciding to write, came about organically as it were,
it wasn't something I had planned.
I have always loved reading and books have
travelled with me everywhere.

As a youngster, my family lived overseas in Kuala
Lumpur. My grandmother used to send (from the UK)
rolled-up comics every week for my sister and I.

The comics were the highlight of the week!
I can never forget Dennis The Menace,
Desperate Dan and Beryl The Peril!

Tales From Over the Moon series

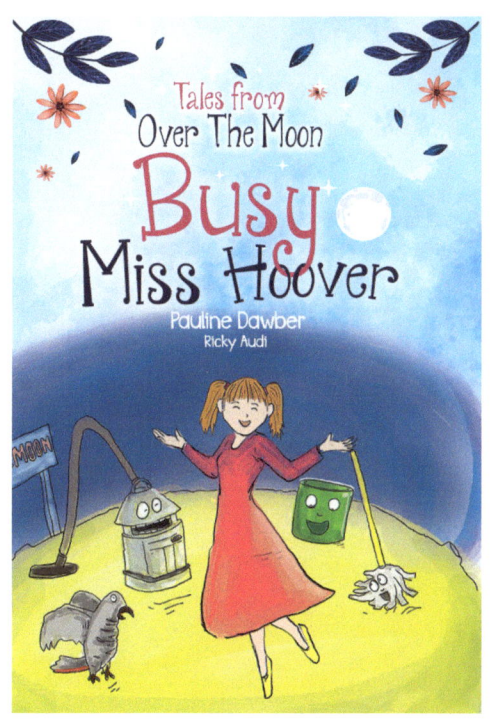

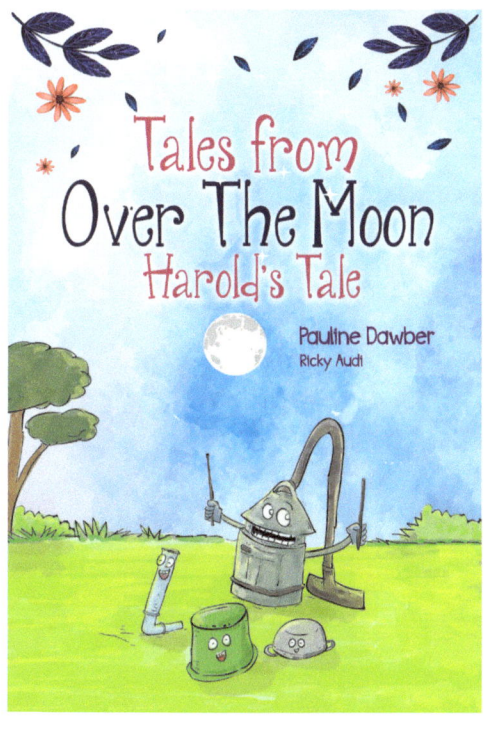

Tales From Over the Moon series

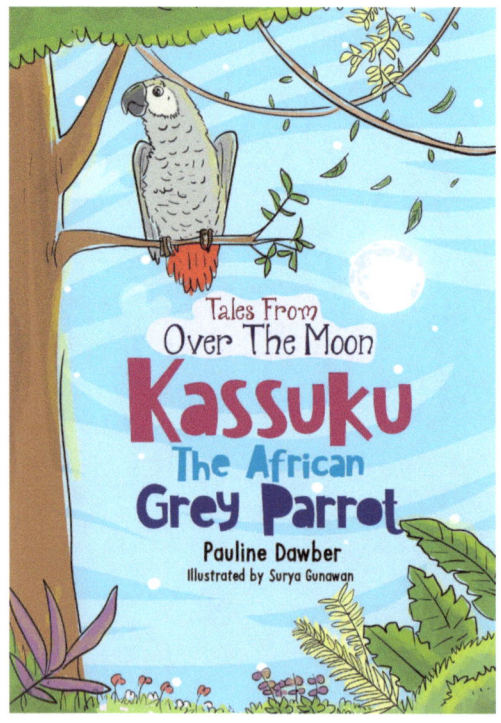
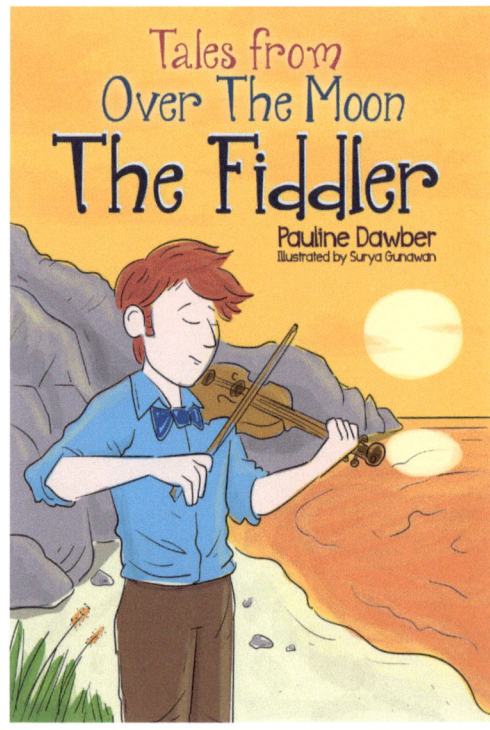

www.ingramcontent.com/pod-product-compliance
Lightning Source LLC
Chambersburg PA
CBHW041822040426
42453CB00005B/132